Forecasting the Weather

Contents

All Kinds of Weather   2

Predicting the Weather   6

Bad Weather   10

Index   16

All Kinds of Weather

There are many kinds of weather.
Weather can be hot, cold, wet, or dry.

Sometimes the sky changes
from sunny to cloudy to rainy.

When we wake up,
we want to know
what the weather will be like.
We want to know if we need to take
a coat or an umbrella.

We can find out by looking
at a weather forecast.

If there's a strong chance of rain,
we can be prepared so we don't get wet.

Predicting the Weather

How do weather forecasters know
what the weather will be like?
They use special tools
to help them predict the weather.

A rain gauge tells how
much rain is falling.

A barometer shows
air pressure.

A weather vane shows the way the wind is blowing.

A thermometer tells how hot or cold it is.

Weather stations tell us
things about the weather.

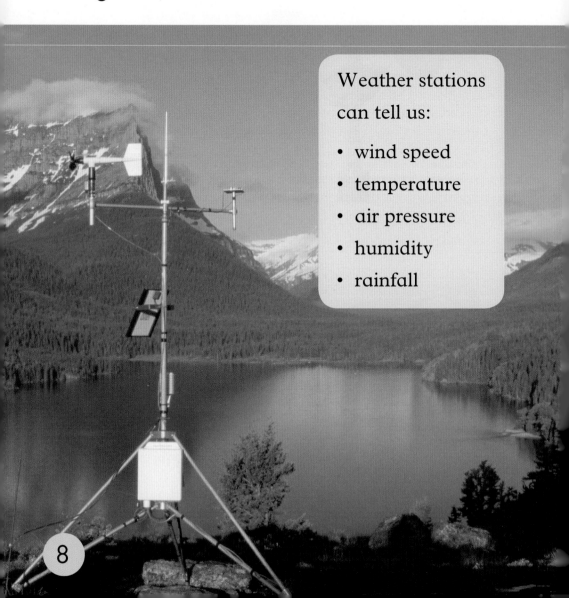

Weather stations
can tell us:

- wind speed
- temperature
- air pressure
- humidity
- rainfall

Some weather stations are in space.

Weather satellites take pictures
of the clouds and the air below,
and show us how weather moves.

Bad Weather

Sometimes long strips of spinning air form in a storm.
The long strips move through the sky.
A tornado is a spinning strip of air that hits the ground.

Tornadoes begin in thunderstorms.

A cloud turns slowly.

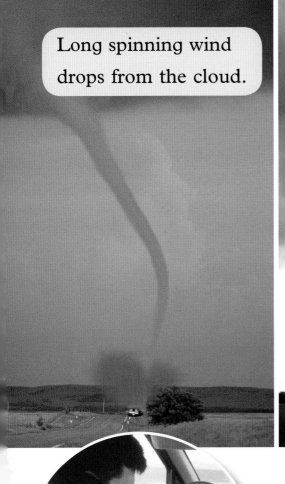

Long spinning wind drops from the cloud.

A tornado picks up dust. This makes it easy to see.

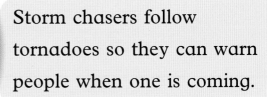

Storm chasers follow tornadoes so they can warn people when one is coming.

Another bad storm is a hurricane.
In a hurricane, the wind blows
very hard.
Hurricanes start over water.

Some pilots fly into hurricanes so they can study them.

Hurricanes can cause a lot of damage.

People put boards on windows to protect them from strong winds.

We need to know when
these bad storms are coming.
Then we can stock up on supplies
or go to a safer place.

13

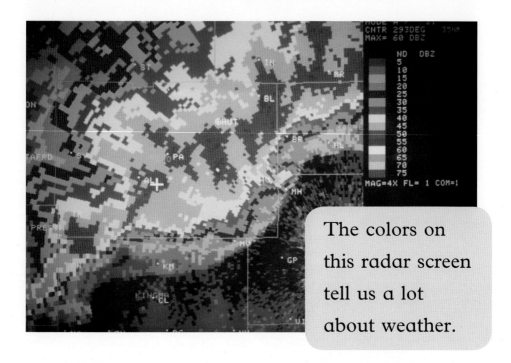

The colors on this radar screen tell us a lot about weather.

People who study weather use their tools to tell how fast the wind is blowing and how much rain is falling.
The tools tell them if they need to warn us about a bad storm.

We see different kinds of weather
all the time.
Thanks to the people who study
the weather, we can plan our day
around it.

Index

barometer	6
hurricane	12
rain gauge	6
storm chasers	11
thermometer	7
tornado	10–11
weather satellite	9
weather stations	8–9
weather vane	7

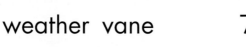